A Color Clown Comes to Town

by Jane Belk Moncure
illustrated by Linda Hohag
and Lori Jacobson

Published by

THE CHILD'S WORLD®

Mankato, Minnesota

The Library —
A Magic Castle

Come to the magic castle
When you are growing tall.
Rows upon rows of Word Windows
Line every single wall.
They reach up high,
As high as the sky,
And you want to open them all.
For every time you open one,
A new adventure has begun.

Laura opens a Word Window.

Guess what
Laura sees?

A funny clown.

"Hi," says the clown.

"I am the color clown. I paint things all over town. You can paint too."

Clown takes the red bucket off his head.
"Let's paint something red," he says.

Clown finds a polar bear.
"Let's paint the bear."

"No! No!" says Laura. "I never saw
a red polar bear. Let's not paint
the polar bear red."

Laura finds an old fire engine.
Would you paint a fire engine red?

They do. They paint it,
and it looks like new.

"Now let's paint something blue,"
says Color Clown.

He finds an igloo.

"No! No!" says Laura. "I never saw a blue igloo. Let's not paint the igloo blue."

Laura finds an old truck. Can you paint a truck blue?

They do! They paint the truck, and it looks like new.

"Now let's paint something yellow," says Color Clown. He finds a snowman in the snow.

"No, no, silly fellow. A snowman is never yellow," says Laura.

Laura finds an old steam shovel.
Would you paint a steam shovel yellow?

They do. They paint it, and it looks
like new.

"Now what can we do?" asks Laura.

"Watch me do tricks," says Color Clown.

He mixes a little red with yellow.
What new color does Clown make?

"I can paint something orange,"
Laura says. What does Laura paint?

"Can you do another trick?" she asks.

"Yes," says Color Clown as he does a flip.

Then Clown mixes a little yellow and blue.

What new color does he make?

"I can paint something green for you," Laura says.

What does Laura paint?

"Can you do another trick?" Laura asks.

"Yes," says Color Clown as he stands on his head.

Then the clown mixes blue with red.

What new color does he make?

"Now I can paint something purple, blue, green, red, yellow, and orange for you," says Laura.

Laura paints a rainbow.

Then Laura says, "Bye-bye, Clown.

It is time to go. I must close this
Word Window."

When Laura gets home, guess what she paints.

A rainbow.

So can you.

You can read these words with Laura.

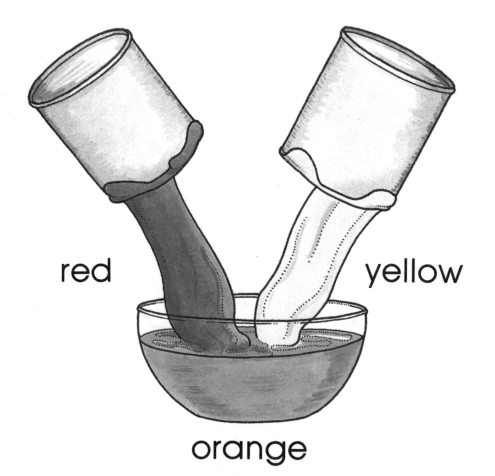

red

yellow

orange